*GREATER THAN A TOURIST BOOKS ARE ALSO AVAILABLE IN EBOOK AND AUDIOBOOK FORMAT.

Greater Than a Tourist Book Series Reviews from Readers

I think the series is wonderful and beneficial for tourists to get information before visiting the city.

-Seckin Zumbul, Izmir Turkey

I am a world traveler who has read many trip guides but this one really made a difference for me. I would call it a heartfelt creation of a local guide expert instead of just a guide.

-Susy, Isla Holbox, Mexico

New to the area like me, this is a must have!

-Joe, Bloomington, USA

This is a good series that gets down to it when looking for things to do at your destination without having to read a novel for just a few ideas.

-Rachel, Monterey, USA

D1469049

Good information to have to plan my trip to this destination.

-Pennie Farrell, Mexico

Great ideas for a port day.

-Mary Martin USA

Aptly titled, you won't just be a tourist after reading this book. You'll be greater than a tourist!

-Alan Warner, Grand Rapids, USA

Even though I only have three days to spend in San Miguel in an upcoming visit, I will use the author's suggestions to guide some of my time there. An easy read - with chapters named to guide me in directions I want to go.

-Robert Catapano, USA

Great insights from a local perspective! Useful information and a very good value!

-Sarah, USA

This series provides an in-depth experience through the eyes of a local. Reading these series will help you to travel the city in with confidence and it'll make your journey a unique one.

-Andrew Teoh, Ipoh, Malaysia

GREATER THAN A TOURIST- MARRAKECH MOROCCO

50 Travel Tips from a Local

Ashley Griefenhagen

The statements in this book are of the authors and may not be the views of
CZYK Publishing or Greater Than a Tourist.
First Edition
Cover designed by: Ivana Stamenkovic
Cover Image: https://pixabay.com/photos/marrakech-minaret-mosque-2285790/

Image 1: By Keirn OConnor from New York City, United States - El Badi
Palace in Marrakesh 2Uploaded by Kurpfalzbilder.de, CC BY-SA 2.0,
https://commons.wikimedia.org/w/index.php?curid=6714962
Image 2: By Acp - Own work, CC BY-SA 3.0,
https://commons.wikimedia.org/w/index.php?curid=593692
Image 3: By Doyler79 at English Wikipedia, CC BY 3.0,
https://commons.wikimedia.org/w/index.php?curid=17775437
Image 4: By Bernard Gagnon - Own work, CC BY-SA 3.0,
https://commons.wikimedia.org/w/index.php?curid=5495055

CZYK Publishing Since 2011.
CZYKPublishing.com
Greater Than a Tourist
Lock Haven, PA
All rights reserved.

ISBN: 9798739101891

>TOURIST

50 TRAVEL TIPS FROM A LOCAL

BOOK DESCRIPTION

With travel tips and culture in our guidebooks written by a local, it is never too late to visit Marrakech Morocco. *Greater Than a Tourist- Marrakech Morocco* by Author *Ashley Griefenhagen* offers the inside scoop on the red city.

Most travel books tell you how to travel like a tourist. Although there is nothing wrong with that, as part of the 'Greater Than a Tourist' series, this book will give you candid travel tips from someone who has lived at your next travel destination. This guide book will not tell you exact addresses or store hours but instead gives you knowledge that you may not find in other smaller print travel books. Experience cultural, culinary delights, and attractions with the guidance of a Local. Slow down and get to know the people with this invaluable guide. By the time you finish this book, you will be eager and prepared to discover new activities at your next travel destination.

Inside this travel guide book you will find:

Visitor information from a Local
Tour ideas and inspiration
Save time with valuable guidebook information

Greater Than a Tourist- A Travel Guidebook with 50 Travel Tips from a Local. Slow down, stay in one place, and get to know the people and culture. By the time you finish this book, you will be eager and prepared to travel to your next destination.

OUR STORY

Traveling is a passion of the Greater than a Tourist book series creator. Lisa studied abroad in college, and for their honeymoon Lisa and her husband toured Europe. During her travels to Malta, an older man tried to give her some advice based on his own experience living on the island since he was a young boy. She was not sure if she should talk to the stranger but was interested in his advice. When traveling to some places she was wary to talk to locals because she was afraid that they weren't being genuine. Through her travels, Lisa learned how much locals had to share with tourists. Lisa created the Greater Than a Tourist book series to help connect people with locals. A topic that locals are very passionate about sharing.

TABLE OF CONTENTS

DEDICATION

This book is dedicated to my wonderful husband. Without you, I would've never gotten the chance to step out of my comfort zone and see the true beauty of Morocco. You have given me a beautiful life and I look forward to many more years together.

ABOUT THE AUTHOR

Ashley is a wife and teacher who was born in Minnesota. She decided to move to Morocco in 2019 to build a new life with her husband, where she still lives today. In her free time, she loves to draw, travel, and spend time outdoors.

HOW TO USE THIS BOOK

The *Greater Than a Tourist* book series was written by someone who has lived in an area for over three months. The goal of this book is to help travelers either dream or experience different locations by providing opinions from a local. The author has made suggestions based on their own experiences. Please check before traveling to the area in case the suggested places are unavailable.

Travel Advisories: As a first step in planning any trip abroad, check the Travel Advisories for your intended destination.
https://travel.state.gov/content/travel/en/traveladvisories/traveladvisories.html

FROM THE PUBLISHER

Traveling can be one of the most important parts of a person's life. The anticipation and memories that you have are some of the best. As a publisher of the Greater Than a Tourist, as well as the popular *50 Things to Know* book series, we strive to help you learn about new places, spark your imagination, and inspire you. Wherever you are and whatever you do I wish you safe, fun, and inspiring travel.

Lisa Rusczyk Ed. D.
CZYK Publishing

WELCOME TO
> TOURIST

El Badi Palace

In winter, the Atlas mountains typically are covered in snow and ice.

Medina walls of Marrakesh

Saadian garden pavilion of the Menara gardens

"With age, comes wisdom. With travel, comes understanding."

– Sandra Lake

Marrakech, Morocco is an amazing place to visit. From the lively atmosphere to the calm tranquility of the gardens, Marrakech is sure to please everyone. I have lived in Morocco for 1.5 years so far, and I have never felt happier. I hope that you visit soon to experience its true beauty for yourself!

Marrakesh
Morocco

Marrakesh
Morocco
Climate

	High	Low
January	66	43
February	69	46
March	74	50
April	77	54
May	83	58
June	91	63
July	99	69
August	99	70
September	91	66
October	82	60
November	73	51
December	68	45

GreaterThanaTourist.com

Temperatures are in Fahrenheit degrees.
Source: NOAA

ATTRACTIONS

1. WALK THROUGH THE NARROW STREETS OF JEMAA EL-FNA

I always tell people that if there's only one thing you're able to see during your trip to Marrakech, go to Jemaa el-Fna. This huge marketplace is only about two and a half miles from the airport, making it the perfect place to visit your first day in town.

When you enter, you'll be overwhelmed by the sights, sounds, and smells coming from every direction. If you're feeling hungry, there is no shortage of food. Everywhere you look, a restaurant or food stand is waiting for you. Whether you're in the mood for a Moroccan tajine or a cheeseburger, I guarantee you'll be able to satisfy your cravings.

I recommend the un-named juice stall deep into Jemaa el-Fna that makes the best juice I have ever tasted. You have your choice of basically any fruit you can imagine. If you'd like, you can get a strawberry-pineapple-avocado smoothie.

If you're a shopper like myself, then you'll be happy to know there are hundreds of shops selling clothes, beauty products, souvenirs, and more. Some shops are more conservative, selling only traditional Moroccan clothing, while other shops are very modern. You'll even be able to find an outfit for a night of clubbing if you wish.

On top of all this, there are hair salons, spas, tailors, hotels, and more hidden within the walls of Jemaa el-Fna.

Be aware that you must bargain for nearly everything in Jemaa el-Fna. While some vendors speak English, some do not, so I recommend learning some Darija (Moroccan Arabic) or going with a trusted tour guide.

2. EXPLORE THE BEAUTY OF BAHIA PALACE

Into Moroccan architecture? If so, you'll love Bahia Palace. This beautiful palace has been on display for the public since the late 19th century and has been a popular tourist attraction ever since. Once you step inside, you'll understand why!

This attraction is made almost entirely of colorfully patterned tiles, from the ground to the ceiling. There are also numerous fountains scattered throughout the entire place, filling the atmosphere with the relaxing sound of flowing water.

If you're looking for somewhere in Marrakech to do a photo shoot, this is it, so be sure to bring your camera with you. Color and greenery are everywhere, making it very Instagram-worthy. Wear bright yellow or blue if you want to match the scenery, and white if you want to contrast it.

My personal favorite is the calmness of the palace. Marrakech is known for being a busy city that never stops moving, so this is a perfect place to escape for a little while and clear your head. The good news is that you don't even have to go very far, since it is located only three miles from the airport.

3. GO SHOPPING AT MENARA MALL

If you want to shop but you're not in the mood for bargaining, then Menara Mall is the place for you. The mall has four stories. The lower level is a supermarket called "Carrefour", while the second floor is made up of shops. Some may sound familiar, such as Zara and H&M. The third floor is filled with restaurants and fast food, such as Burger King and

Dominos. Lastly, the fourth floor is an arcade "Kidzo" which is perfect for little ones! They have plenty of games and even bumper cars. In front of Menara Mall is also full of more restaurants if you would like to sit back and grab lunch while you admire the view of the city. They even have "Chili's" if you need a break from Moroccan food and want a taste of home.

4. GO FOR A SWIM IN ESSAOURIA

I love Marrakech, but one downside of the city is that it doesn't have any beaches. However, the good news is that beautiful beaches are less than a three hours drive away. Essaouira is a breezy city located about 103 miles away from Marrakech. Here, you can enjoy a nice sunny day at "Plage d'Essaouira", one of Essaouira's most famous beaches. Since the beach can be quite windy, surfing and kite-boarding are very popular, so don't forget your surfboard!

If water sports aren't your thing, there is also the amazing opportunity to ride camels next to the beach. I would especially recommend this to couples, as I rode one with my husband and found it to be a very fun, romantic experience. However, be careful while getting on and off the camels. They're much larger than you might expect!

Another personal favorite of mine is the souk (marketplace) in Essaouira. This souk is similar to Jemaa el-Fna, but much less crowded. They have all of the same things (souvenirs, clothes, home decor, etc) and they're oftentimes a cheaper price as well.

NIGHTLIFE

5. WATCH A LIVE PERFORMANCE AT THEATRO

Are you looking for a place to let go and have a few drinks? Maybe watch some live performances? Then I would recommend one of the most famous nightclubs in Marrakech; Theatro.

This nightclub is anything but ordinary. As soon as you enter, you'll be immediately shocked by the bright colors, vibrant makeup, and crazy costumes. Theatro also has exciting performances nearly every single night, ranging from singers and dancers to acrobatics. And of course, a full drink menu is available. One thing is for sure, you will never get bored here!

6. LET GO AT THE 555 CLUB

If you're just looking for a good place to dance and drink, then the 555 club is for you. This nightclub has a huge dance floor with a wide variety of drink options and great DJs. There is also a rooftop lounge upstairs called "Sky Bar" if you're looking for a quieter place to have a drink. They have a large menu of food as well, including tapas, sandwiches, desserts, and more.

7. ENJOY A NIGHT OUT AT THE VIP ROOM

The VIP room is one of my favorite nightclubs in Morocco and was even voted travelers choice 2020 by Tripadvisor. The dance floor, lighting, and music are all amazing! They also have a great alcohol and champagne menu. One of the best parts about VIP room is that they frequently have events, such as ladies' night, "Madness Saturday" and more.

WHERE TO STAY

8. STAY IN A RIAD STRAIGHT OUT OF A MOVIE SCENE

When you imagine Morocco, it's hard not to think of a Moroccan Riad. Riad literally means 'garden' in Arabic, but it's more commonly known as a traditional Moroccan house or hotel. These gorgeous Andalusian-style houses are built around a garden that usually covers the entire ground floor, while the upstairs is reserved for the bedrooms and bathrooms.

Upper-end Riads usually have fantastic amenities, such as spas, restaurants, and rooftop pools. There's nothing like going for a swim on a 100-degree day while admiring the view of the red city. There is also 24-hour staff, so be sure to order a drink while you're enjoying your swim.

I must note that Riads can be more expensive than other hotels in the area. However, they're still not much more than a typical American hotel. There are plenty of Riads, modest or luxurious, throughout Marrakech so be sure to do your research and find what best works for you.

9. ENJOY THE CONVENIENCE OF A MODERN HOTEL

Hotels are perfect if you're looking for a comfortable, familiar travel experience. They're also fairly inexpensive and usually located next to a variety of bars, restaurants, and stores. I would recommend this option to families because they almost always have a swimming pool (or even a small waterpark). Arcades and bowling alleys are sometimes included too.

10. ENJOY THE INDEPENDENCE OF AN AIRBNB

Staying in an Airbnb is by far my favorite option. You can get an entire apartment to yourself for less money than you would spend on a hotel. Airbnb's in Marrakech usually have swimming pools and a security guard as well.

The only downside is that there isn't any room service or staff to help you. However, I've found that the hosts are typically more than willing to assist you with anything you may need. Personally, I enjoy the independence of renting my own apartment and doing things on my own terms.

Another overlooked benefit of staying in an Airbnb is that you have a fully equipped kitchen that you can use at any time. If you're an experienced traveler, then you know that eating out every day can get expensive. Having your own kitchen lets you make your own meals and save a lot of money that can be used for other activities. Maybe you can even try your hand at some local dishes!

LIVE LIKE A LOCAL

11. UNWIND AT A HAMMAM

While visiting foreign places, people often like to stay in their "tourist bubble", but have you ever lived like a local? In my opinion, you never truly get to know a country until you step out of your comfort zone. If you feel like you're ready to make the leap, then my first recommendation would be to visit a hammam.

Moroccan hammams are essentially public bathhouses, similar to saunas, that Moroccans swear by and usually visit once a week. They're separated by gender and consist of at least three rooms, varying in temperature from warm to steaming. Most people start in the "warm" room and then gradually move their way to the hottest room, but it's your choice where you would like to stay.

So, you've settled in and you're ready to get started. Now what? First, you need to get undressed. On the female side, women typically get completely naked and on the male side, men wear swim shorts. If you're a female and uncomfortable getting naked in front of strangers (I don't blame you!), it's okay to wear a bathing suit.

Next, it's time to exfoliate. You can either do this by yourself or you can pay the "kessala" (the person working there whose job is literally to scrub) to do it for you. If you choose to use the kessala, they will lather an exfoliation glove with soap and scrub your entire body. Be aware that they can sometimes scrub super harshly! Lastly, you can rinse off and continue, as usual, washing your hair or whatever else you may need to do. After you leave, you'll feel like a whole new person!

12. RELAX AT THE CAFÉ

Morocco's favorite pastime is, by far, cafes. They're very convenient because they usually have food, wifi, and large TV screens. Whether you want to grab a bite to eat, discuss a business proposal, watch a football match, or just chat with friends, the cafe is the place to go.

Cafes are found everywhere in Marrakech, so you'll have no trouble finding one. Keep in mind that cafes are mostly filled with men, but that is changing with time. I recommend cafes in the neighborhood "Gueliz" since most of them are mixed and have more of a modern feel to them. They also tend to have a bigger variety of foods and drinks.

13. GET A HENNA TATTOO

Henna is one of those things that is a symbol of Morocco. It is done for most celebrations, such as weddings, birthdays, the birth of a new baby, and more. It is also popular among tourists.

So, what exactly is Henna? It is a brownish-red dye that comes from plants and is completely natural. Women use it to make intricate designs on their skin and it can even be used as a hair dye since it even has the ability to turn hair red. Henna is mostly done on the hands and feet and it lasts for at least two weeks.

If you're interested in getting one of these beautiful temporary tattoos, I would recommend going to Jemma el-Fna for a fast and easy experience. Jemaa el-Fna has several women just after the entrance that can apply henna for you. They'll give you a book to look through and you can choose whichever design you like. There are also women called "nakasha" who will come to your home and apply any henna design that you would like. Be aware that it can tickle!

When I first visited Morocco, my sister-in-law gave me henna and I loved it. It has such a unique look to it that receives a lot of compliments. After I returned home, everyone was asking me where I got my henna done!

WHAT TO BRING

14. MEDICINE

Morocco has tons of pharmacies that have plenty of medicine available, so you don't need to bring much with you. You can even just buy antibiotics at the pharmacy without going to the doctor, unlike in the US.

However, if you're a creature of habit, I recommend taking your own medicine with you. Even if you can find similar products in Morocco, you won't find the same exact thing. Also, it might be a good idea to bring anti-nausea and anti-diarrhea pills in case you have a bad reaction to the new food.

15. BEAUTY AND FEMININE PRODUCTS

For women, there are a few things I recommend bringing with you since they can be hard to find in Morocco.

Firstly, I would bring women's shaving cream. For some odd reason, I've never seen this sold here in Marrakech, though they do sell men's. Secondly, bring your own tampons/pads. Tampons are sometimes sold in major supermarkets like Marjane and Carrefour but they have a very limited selection. Pads are also sold everywhere but again, the selection isn't great.

16. CLOTHING

What kind of clothing you should bring all depends on when you'll be visiting. The temperature can vary a lot throughout the seasons, though it's always quite warm in Marrakech.

Keep in mind that the summertime can be scorching, even reaching 115 degrees at times! With this being said, be sure to pack light, flowy clothing that will keep you cool. It's also a good idea to bring good shoes that won't hurt your feet. Marrakech generally doesn't have the best roads and it's easy to trip, so be careful.

For the wintertime, I recommend bringing a variety of items and dressing in layers. The daytime can be quite warm but after the sun goes down, it can get cold really quickly. Light jackets and sweaters are a perfect choice for the wintertime, in my opinion.

WHERE TO GROCERY SHOP

17. GET FRESH PRODUCE FROM THE MEN ON THE STREET

One way that Morocco differs from the western world is that there are people all over the streets selling various things from their cars/trucks or even just by hand. The most common is fruits and vegetables. All you need to do is leave your doorstep and you have a mini supermarket right in front of you! I like this because it's the cheapest and freshest option. However, you will have to do a bit of bargaining since there aren't fixed prices. Also, be sure to wash your fruits and vegetables thoroughly!

18. BUY FROM THE STORES ON THE STREET

Another way to shop is from the small stores called "hanoot". These are everywhere. I've even seen more than two on the same street! Groceries here are slightly more expensive than from the sellers on the street, however, there is typically a larger variety of fruits and vegetables. Meat, dairy, and spices are often sold here as well. Be aware that you will still need to bargain in most stores.

19. BUY FROM THE SUPERMARKET

Supermarkets are great for those who don't want to bargain and for those who want a huge selection of items. There are fewer supermarkets than there are hanoots but, don't worry! There are still plenty of them around Marrakech. The three most common are Marjane, Carrefour, and BIM.

Marjane is the most common, with there being at least one in nearly every neighborhood of Marrakech. You can find pretty much everything here, even clothing and electronics. Some American food is sold here as well. Cereal, peanut butter, and Ben & Jerry's ice cream are a few things that I've seen.

Carrefour is another common supermarket. It is a French company, so the products differ slightly from Marjane. Carrefour typically has an even bigger selection and more American snacks and beauty products. You are guaranteed to find everything you need here!

BIM is a smaller supermarket so the selection isn't as great as Marjane or Carrefour. They sell very few fruits and vegetables, however, they have basic things like milk, cheese, and bread. They also have a lot of snacks, like chips and candy. Think of BIM like a convenient store, it's good for when you're in a rush and just need one thing!

WHERE TO EAT

20. CHOW DOWN ON SOME CLASSIC AMERICAN FOOD

Marrakech is one of the best places to go if you're craving American food. Nearly every restaurant or cafe will have some American items on the menu, such as cheeseburgers and fries. On top of that, there are plenty of restaurants that are dedicated to American food!

One place that I always recommend is called "Le Warner" on Avenue Yacoub El Marini in Gueliz. This restaurant is unique because it's 1950's themed. All of the decorations, music, and uniforms will make you feel like you're in a retro American diner! Plus, the food is amazing. They have cheeseburgers, milkshakes, cheesecake, hot dogs, and much more. Also, I have always found the servers to be quick and kind.

Another restaurant worth checking out is "The GoodBun" on Rue du Sergent Levet in Gueliz. This place only has cheeseburgers, fries, milkshakes, and a few desserts but they're extremely good at what they do. They make some of the best cheeseburgers and milkshakes that I've ever tasted. Also, you can top your burger with quite a few different toppings if you wish.

21. ENJOY THE BEST MOROCCAN FOOD THAT MARRAKECH HAS TO OFFER

In my opinion, if you want the best Moroccan meals, you have to eat it at someone's house since it's very fresh and always made from scratch. However, I realize this isn't always possible. The good news is that amazing Moroccan restaurants are everywhere!

The first place that I recommend is called "Al Fassia" on Boulevard Mohamed Zerktouni in Gueliz. They have all of the delicious traditional Moroccan dishes here, such as tajine, couscous, pastilla, and more. The atmosphere is calm and intimate, and the interior is beautiful as well. Keep in mind that it is formal and somewhat pricey. In my opinion, Al Fassia would be perfect for a special romantic dinner.

Another amazing choice is Dar L'hssira on Rue Tachenbacht (about five minutes away from Koutoubia Mosque). This tiny restaurant might not look like much from the outside, but looks can be deceiving! It is absolutely delicious on the inside, serving tajine and couscous as well as plenty of beverage options. It is informal and inexpensive as well, making it the perfect place to take your children for lunch or to simply just hang out!

22. CHECK OUT ALL THE OPTIONS

Are you sick of only eating Moroccan or American food and want a change? Well, you'll be happy to know that Morocco has quite a diverse selection of food. Italian is the most common cuisine, but there are a few others as well.

"Cosy Pasta" is an excellent choice for great Italian food in Marrakech. It is located on Avenue Yacoub El Mansour in Gueliz. Here, you can build your own pasta from scratch which is a unique option I haven't seen anywhere else. First, you start with what kind of noodles you want, then sauce, then lastly, the cheese. You can also add extras. This is a tasty and inexpensive restaurant that is perfect for a quick lunch!

Good Asian food can be hard to find in Morocco, but I highly recommend "Wok To Walk" in Carre Eden mall. Similar to Cosy Pasta, you can build your own entree. You're able to choose what kind of meat you want, then vegetables, then sauce, as well as extras. I found their food to be very good and inexpensive.

HOW TO GET AROUND

23. BUSES

There are plenty of buses that go to every single area of Marrakech. The buses all have numbers that correspond to each city, so make sure to know the number beforehand. Keep in mind that these buses are often cramped and can get quite hot in the summer. However, they're super inexpensive. They're convenient as well because you can quickly pay inside the bus with cash or card and they're everywhere. Just wait at any bus stop and you'll see one shortly.

If you're interested in taking a bus to different cities, then you have more options. First, there are standard buses. These can get quite cramped and hot as well, but they're still more comfortable than the city buses and they're inexpensive. For these, you just need to go to one of the bus stations in Marrakech and find what times they're leaving. Then, you can either pay at the station or inside of the bus.

Another option is taking one of the more luxurious buses. These are slightly more expensive, but they usually have air conditioning, wifi, more legroom and they're cleaner. A popular bus company that I would recommend is called "Supratours". They have a website where you can even pay online ahead of time. Of course, you can visit the bus station too if you prefer to do it that way!

24. TAXIS

If there's one thing you'll never find a shortage of in Morocco, it's taxis! Taxis are everywhere you look, which makes them the main mode of transportation for both locals and tourists.

There are both petit taxis and grand taxis. Petit taxis will take you anywhere in Marrakech, while grand taxis will take you to other cities. Petit taxis have a maximum of three people, while grand taxis have a maximum of six, so plan accordingly for large groups.

If you want to leave Marrakech, you will need to go to the taxi station near Jemma el-Fna. Then, you can pay the man at the station and wait for the remaining five people to gather. If there are empty seats, you can pay for them if you don't want to wait and/or you want more room.

25. TRAINS

For traveling to faraway cities, a train might be your best option. They are generally very quick, clean, and comfortable. They're not too expensive either!

For Marrakech, the train station is located in Gueliz. There, you can view the departure schedule and pay. The station has a McDonald's as well, so you can grab a bite to eat while you wait.

Another option is purchasing your ticket online beforehand. I recommend doing it this way because you are almost guaranteed a good seat when you board and fares are often cheaper.

26. RENT A CAR

Renting a car is another popular option for obvious reasons! You have much more independence with no restricting schedules.

You can rent a car ahead of time through a website like Kayak or there's plenty of car renting companies within Morocco as well. Just be sure that they're legit and make sure they're not overcharging you. A popular rental agency is called "Sixt," located in Gueliz. They're trustworthy and have a wide variety of vehicles.

If you rent a car, keep in mind that driving can be a little "crazy" in Morocco compared to the US or other places. Drivers don't always respect the rules and just want to get where they're going quickly. There are also motorcycles, horses, donkeys, and more on the roads at all times. Be sure to always stay very alert! If you're a nervous driver like me, I recommend using another mode of transportation.

CRIME AND SAFETY

27. PICKPOCKETING

Morocco is an extremely safe country. Serious crimes happen very rarely, so there's no need to be scared about visiting. However, petty crimes like pickpocketing do happen, especially in bigger cities like Marrakech.

While visiting Morocco as a tourist, be aware that you'll be a "target" for pickpocketing. Unfortunately, they see that you're a foreigner and think that you have tons of cash in your pockets.

For storing money, I recommend using something like a fanny pack or a crossbody that goes across your body. Make sure to keep the zipper in front of you and keep the bag tightly secured. Also, don't get distracted, and always try to stay alert and aware of your surroundings. Crowded places like Jemaa el-Fna are notorious for pickpocketing, so take extra caution in those areas.

If you do end up getting pickpocketed, it doesn't hurt to go to the police. They take these crimes seriously, especially if it happens to a tourist.

They might even be able to get your money or items back to you.

28. THEFT

Theft is another somewhat common crime in Marrakech. From what I've seen, most criminals only want your money/phone, etc, and will not do any harm to you, so don't be alarmed.

The most common form of theft is a woman getting her bag stolen. Usually, one or two men will spot her and rip her bag off of her shoulder. They also frequently use a motorcycle to get away quickly, so be extra careful of these. Another common form of theft that happens is a man or woman getting their phone stolen right out of their hands. Criminals use special "tricks" for this, like approaching you on the street, seeming to be very nice and friendly. Then while you're distracted, they'll take your phone and run.

Theft mostly happens at night, so I wouldn't recommend walking around after dark, especially if you're alone. If you must, avoid dark and empty streets.

If you do get something stolen from you, definitely go to the police. They will take it very seriously and you'll file a police report. I'm almost certain that they can find your items, too.

29. OVERCHARGING

Being overcharged is probably the most common thing that happens to tourists in Marrakech. Sadly, whether you're trying to get a taxi or buy some things at the store, many people will try to get as much money as they can from you.

The easiest way to combat this is to go with a trusted Moroccan friend or a tour guide. It would be good to learn some basic Darija (Moroccan Arabic), especially numbers so that you can negotiate. Also, be sure to learn the prices of basic things like snacks and clothing. Always keep in mind that things in Morocco will usually cost much less than they do in the US!

30. HARASSMENT

If you're a woman visiting Morocco, harassment will be an annoying thing that you have to deal with quite frequently. Unfortunately, harassment is a big problem in Morocco, especially Marrakech and it can be very overwhelming.

The most common thing that happens is men coming up and complimenting you or asking for your phone number. Usually, it's nothing scary and they'll leave you alone after you ignore them or tell them no.

If you really want to avoid this, you can dress more modestly and avoid things like shorts and tank tops. You can even cover your head if you want to. However, it all depends on your comfort level, and keep in mind that some amount of harassment will probably happen no matter what, but it doesn't have to ruin your trip.

If a man comes up to you, my advice is to just keep walking and not even make eye contact. If a man is being persistent or making you uncomfortable, then I recommend being affirmative and don't be afraid to say no. You can also go to the police and report the man. Like other crimes, police take harassment seriously and the man will most likely get in trouble.

THE DIFFERENCE BETWEEN CITIES, TOWNS, AND VILLAGES

31. CITIES

What a lot of people don't realize about Morocco is that it's full of huge, bustling cities that are extremely modern. When visiting a major city in Morocco, you will see plenty of luxury apartments and sports cars. Some of the biggest cities are: Casablanca (population of 3 million), Rabat (population of 1.5 million), Fes (population of 964,000), Marrakech (population of 840,000), Agadir (population of 700,000) and Tangier (population of 690,000).

Cities in Morocco tend to have "everything", making them the most common places for tourists to visit or for expats to move to. They typically have tons of supermarkets, bars, restaurants, malls, and more all within a short walk or drive. Another important thing to know about cities is that they have much better hospitals and healthcare than towns or villages.

Of course, there are a couple of downsides. Firstly, cities generally have a higher crime rate, but this is true everywhere. Besides, the crime rate for every major city in Morocco is still significantly low compared to cities in the rest of the world. Secondly, they're more crowded and don't have a lot of green space. However, you can still find plenty of parks in cities, and maybe even beaches or mountains as well depending on the city.

32. TOWNS

Towns are generally smaller than cities, but they're still much bigger than villages. Here, you can live comfortably with all of your basic needs met. There are supermarkets, cafes, and more. The nice thing about towns is that there's plenty of green space, they're less crowded, they have lower crime rates and the cost of renting an apartment or getting a hotel room is significantly cheaper.

However, there's a lot less to do. It's rare to find a restaurant in a town. There are only cafes, which are still mostly 90% men. Also, you will need to travel further to get to places. I wouldn't recommend staying in a town for long since it would start to become difficult for a tourist. However, many towns have beautiful nature such as waterfalls, parks, and more that would be good to visit for a day trip.

33. VILLAGES

Villages are often quite small and have a more traditional way of living. Most houses are made from clay and have big open spaces where families grow crops and raise animals.

A unique thing about villages is that the community is extremely close-knit. If you need some sugar or just someone to talk to, a neighbor is always there to help you. In the past, a whole village would even share the same stove! Also, most of the people in villages own their own land, making them richer than you may have thought.

The downside of villages is that there aren't many supermarkets, cafes, or anything to do. Also, the quality of education is poor and children might have to walk a very long distance to get to school. However, this is slowly changing. More schools are being built and technology such as TV and cellphones are starting to appear in homes.

Like towns, I wouldn't recommend staying a long time in a village. But, I do recommend visiting one at least once. Even though I had traveled to many places throughout Morocco, I never realized how extremely different people's lives can be until I visited a village. It gave me a whole new insight into Morocco and the world in general.

MOROCCAN FOOD/DRINKS

34. ENJOY A TRADITIONAL TAJINE

Tajine is by far the most popular food in Morocco! Nearly everywhere you go, you'll see tajine pots being sold, or tajine being eaten in restaurants. If you stay in a Moroccan family's home, they'll probably serve you tajine as well. So, what exactly is it?

Tajine is a delicious slow-cooked mixture of meat, vegetables, and spices. The vegetables and meat are typically bought and then cooked on the same day, so it's extremely healthy and fresh. There are two types of tajines: One is with chicken and vegetables such as potatoes, carrots, peas, and more. The other kind is with beef and apricots. After the meat and vegetables are washed and cut, they are put in a cone-shaped pot (also called a tajine). Then, they slowly cook for hours until it softens and a sauce is formed. After it's done cooking, it is served with bread and then the bread is used to scoop up the tajine. Keep in mind that it is never eaten with forks or spoons and in a Moroccan home, everyone eats from the same pot. If you're uncomfortable with this, you can ask for your own plate, of course.

35. TASTE A SPICY COUSCOUS

Couscous is probably the second most popular meal in Morocco. You'll see it on a lot of restaurant menus as well, and it's frequently eaten in Moroccan homes. Traditionally, it's prepared every single Friday.

Couscous is made of vegetables, spices, and of course, couscous (crushed wheat). Couscous is slowly cooked in a special type of pot that has two levels: One for the couscous, and one for the vegetables. While the vegetables are cooking, the steam rises, cooking the couscous as well. Couscous is usually made with chicken or beef, (though other meat can be used as well) and several different kinds of vegetables. Carrots, zucchini, chickpeas, cabbage, and turnips are just a few of the vegetables that I've seen used. The couscous is usually taken out of the pot 2-3 times, crushed, and then put back in the pot to cook again. This is so that it comes out smooth and not chunky. After it's done steaming, it's served on a huge plate. Families eat couscous together by spoon, but some might eat it with their hands.

36. ENJOY SOME FLAKEY MSEMEN FOR BREAKFAST

If you ever have breakfast in Morocco, you're bound to come across Msemen. While it's commonly eaten for breakfast, it can also be served as an afternoon snack or even a dessert. One thing that I love about Msemen is that it's very versatile!

Msemen is a type of flatbread native to North Africa. Think of it like a pancake, but thinner and layered. It is made from flour, semolina, sugar, salt, yeast, and water. First, the dry ingredients are mixed with water. Then, the dough is kneaded until it is elastic. After that, the dough is rolled into balls and then covered with oil. Finally, the balls of dough should be flattened into very thin rectangles and put in a frying pan to cook. The dough should be flipped numerous times in the pan until it is slightly crispy on the outside.

Msemen can be served with butter, cheese, jelly, and much more. My favorite way to eat msemen is with Nutella. It tastes exactly like a crepe! Another way that I enjoy eating msemen is with onions and spices. All ways are delicious, it just depends on if you're in the mood for a spicy or sweet breakfast/snack.

37. DRINK A HOT CUP OF MINT TEA

If you've ever been to Morocco, you'll see that Moroccans are addicted to mint tea. They are constantly drinking it in the cafe and their homes. Some even drink it with every meal!

Mint tea is made from gunpowder tea, sugar, water, and of course, mint. It is really simple and only takes about 10 minutes to prepare. First, the gunpowder tea is added to the teapot and some boiling water is poured in and stirred around with the tea. Then, sugar is added to the mixture (it is usually two teaspoons or more). After that, more boiling water is added and the mint leaves are added in. Finally, the teapot is brought back to the stove for everything to boil together for a while longer.

After the tea is done boiling, it's served in a traditional Moroccan tea set. Something unique about

Moroccan tea is that it's poured from a very high height. This is so that a thick layer of foam forms on the surface of the tea. While it's usually served with sweets, it can be drunk with any meal.

HOLIDAYS

38. EID AL-ADHA

Since Morocco is a Muslim majority country, it mostly celebrates Islamic holidays.

The most popular of these holidays is definitely Eid al-Adha (or 'Eid' for short), which literally means "festival of sacrifice". On this day, Muslims celebrate the famous story of Abraham's willingness to kill his own son, Isaac, but he sacrifices a sheep instead. Yes, this story exists in the Quran as well!

According to Islam, Muslims must buy a sheep and sacrifice it on the day of Eid. However, if they can't afford a sheep, it's perfectly okay to not buy one or do the sacrifice. Also, if they're unable to participate in Eid for whatever reason, they should feed a poor family instead.

Eid al-Adha is celebrated by eating a huge feast, which includes the sacrificed sheep, fruits, vegetables, desserts, and more. (Any meat that is not eaten should be given to a family in need). After this, families exchange gifts, dress up in nice clothing, listen to music, recite the Quran, and more. In my opinion, the celebration of Eid is quite similar to Christmas.

39. RAMADAN

Ramadan is another Islamic holiday, and it's extremely important because it's one of the five pillars of Islam. During Ramadan, Muslims should not eat or drink from sunrise to sunset. This also includes smoking and sexual relations. But why, you might ask?

Well, the main reason is for Muslims to strengthen their relationship with God. It is believed that while fasting, many distractions are lost and one is better able to focus on their faith. Muslims are supposed to pray and recite the Quran more often during Ramadan.

Secondly, it is believed that Ramadan improves one's self-control. Since it is very difficult to abstain from food and drink throughout the entire day (even water), it is a very rewarding feeling when you successfully complete each day of Ramadan. I've been told that many people quit bad habits such as smoking and drinking during Ramadan and feel like they have better control over their lives.

Finally, the Muslim community is strengthened during Ramadan. Families are brought closer because every night of the month, they eat a huge meal together before sunset. This meal is called "iftar" which literally means "breakfast." Also, charity is increased during Ramadan and people are encouraged to give back to their community and provide a meal for those who can't afford it.

While Ramadan might sound extremely difficult, it is important to remember that there are numerous exceptions. If someone is sick, pregnant, breastfeeding, or cannot fast for whatever reason, it is perfectly okay not to participate. Even if someone just simply feels like they can't handle it anymore and they have to eat, it's okay if they do so. If you ask around, most Muslims will tell you that they actually love Ramadan and look forward to it every year!

40. EID AL-FITR

Eid al-Fitr literally means "the festival of breaking the fast" and it's the second Eid that Muslims celebrate. This eid happens on the last day of Ramadan and is the only day in the month where Muslims don't fast. Instead, they prepare a huge feast and eat it together with family. They also wear nice clothing and exchange gifts, similar to Eid al-Adha.

I don't recommend that tourists visit Morocco during Eid or Ramadan. On Eid al-Adha and Eid al-Fitr, everything is completely closed on the day of Eid and usually for a few days after as well. During Ramadan, businesses have limited hours.

41. OTHER HOLIDAYS

Even though Moroccans mainly celebrate Islamic holidays, they sometimes celebrate other ones as well. If a person is very religious, they might steer clear of all non-religious holidays, while a less religious person would probably have no problem celebrating them. I have found a mixture of both in Morocco, but most of them seem to be somewhere in the middle.

You might be surprised to know that many Moroccans celebrate Christmas! Of course, they do it in their own way. They usually combine Christmas and New Years' together and decorate a Christmas tree with ornaments on New Year's Day. They also will sometimes wear "ugly Christmas sweaters", exchange presents, and cook a large meal. Christmas events such as making a gingerbread house are also common in larger cities.

New Year's day is also widely celebrated in Morocco. Some Moroccans go out for drinks with friends while others stay inside and have a small party with family. For New Year's Eve parties, it's customary to buy a cake and enjoy it together. Fireworks are also common! Don't worry, if you visit Morocco during the holidays you'll have plenty of things to do.

CELEBRATIONS

42. WEDDINGS

A Moroccan wedding is a completely surreal experience. They're like nothing you have ever seen before, and are completely different from US weddings, so be prepared for a bit of culture shock if you attend one!

A traditional Moroccan wedding can range anywhere from $1,500 to even $100,000 or more! They're held at large venues and typically have hundreds of guests. There's often plenty of staff who serve the guests, and a woman called a "negaffa" who serves the bride throughout the entire night, constantly checking her clothes and makeup to ensure that she always looks her best.

Unlike American weddings, there's really no ceremony. First, all the guests arrive, eat some treats at the entrance, and get settled at their tables. Then, the bride and groom show up as people cheer and music is played for them. After they enter the venue, the bride and groom are usually separated from each other for most of the night, except for a few moments to take pictures together and dance.

The bride is usually taken first and carried around inside of an elegant type of "chair" with pillars, called an "amaria." Several men carry her around the entire venue while she waves and says hello to guests. Then, the same process is repeated except with the groom.

Next, there is a henna party. The bride changes into a green dress and the Negaffa applies henna to her hand while the guests are watching and taking pictures.

After this, the bride and groom are reunited and everyone sits down with their families to enjoy their meal, which is usually spicy roasted chicken and beef but it can vary a lot.

Finally, the bride and groom cut the cake and then have their first dance as husband and wife while everyone dances along and pictures are taken.

The wedding usually lasts for at least 10 hours and goes well into the morning. I left my wedding at 6 am! So, if you attend a Moroccan wedding make sure to get plenty of sleep the night before and wear comfortable shoes!

43. THE BIRTH OF A BABY

When a baby is first born, family and friends visit the new mother in the hospital. They even stay with her for a few days, helping around the house until she gets back on her feet.

After seven days, a party is thrown for the mother and her baby, similar to a baby shower in the US. The party is called "sbaa" which literally translates to "seven". Friends, family, and even neighbors are invited. Decorations are put up and a huge meal is cooked, usually meat, fruit, cake and much more. Sometimes, even a sheep is slaughtered and cooked for the occasion!

The mother typically receives a lot of money and gifts from guests to help take care of the baby. The gifts are usually necessities rather than things like toys. Blankets, clothes, and diapers are all common presents.

Both women and men attend these parties, but they might separate. Sometimes a sheikh (a religious leader) comes and reads the Quran, wishing good luck and health for the baby. In this case, the men often stay and listen while the women go into a separate room and dance to celebrate the new baby.

But, the women may stay and listen to the Quran if they choose.

The birth of a new baby is a huge deal in Moroccan culture and the entire family gets together to celebrate the event and help the new mother to the best of their ability. If you get the chance to attend one, you'll have a lot of fun and get to see just how close Moroccan families are.

44. HAJJ PARTIES

Hajj literally means "to go on a journey" and is one of the five pillars of Islam. After a person returns from their pilgrimage, a small party is thrown for them to celebrate achieving this huge religious goal.

Hajj is essentially a pilgrimage to Mecca, a city in Saudi Arabia. Every year, millions of Muslims take a trip to Mecca, making it one of the largest gatherings in the world.

The main part of hajj is that Muslims must circulate around the Kaaba 7 times. The Kaaba is a square, black building located in the middle of mosque al-Haram. It is believed that Abraham built the Kaaba, so it is very sacred in Islam.

After a Muslim returns from hajj, their friends and family gather to celebrate. He or she will also often bring gifts back from Mecca to their family. After that, a large meal is prepared and they read the Quran together.

CLOTHING

45. JILLABA

While visiting Morocco, you might be surprised to see that many people appear to be wearing the same thing; a long, loose-fitting gown with long sleeves and a hood. This gown is called a Jillaba, and it's by far the most popular outfit choice for Moroccans. They are unisex, so both women and men wear them.

Jillabas can be made with any type of material, in any color, and with any type of design. Women usually wear Jillabas with decorative beads and flowery designs or geometric patterns. Men tend to wear solid colors or more simple designs, like stripes.

In the winter months, people usually wear clothes under their Jillabas, like fuzzy pajamas to keep them warm. During the summertime, clothing is not usually worn under the Jillaba unless it's thin leggings or something similar.

I highly recommend buying a Jillaba or two while in Morocco. They are an excellent thing to wear while visiting because they are modest and stylish! Locals will appreciate the act as well. They can be bought literally everywhere in Marrakech, from the streets to the malls, so keep your eye out.

46. CAFTAN

Caftans are somewhat similar to Jillabas but are usually only worn in the summertime and they're made from lighter materials (such as cotton). They're unisex as well!

Like Jillabas, Caftans are gowns that can be made from any material with any color or design. However, they're usually simpler than Jillabas and both men and women tend to only wear solid colors or stripes. Things like intricate designs and embroidery are often left out, but not always. Also, they can have long sleeves or short sleeves, and they can also be long or short in length.

Caftans are perfect for the summertime in Morocco since they're very lightweight and cool, so I recommend buying one along with your Jillaba. If you're like me and get hot easily, I would recommend buying a short sleeve ankle-length kaftan to wear during the hotter days. They can be found everywhere and you can even ask a tailor to make you a custom one!

47. TAKCHITA

The Takchita is essentially just a fancier version of the Caftan, except they're not unisex (only women wear them) and you're not likely to see one unless you're at a celebration of some kind.

A standard Takchita has two parts. First, it has a Caftan with tons of embroidery and jewels. Then, it has a robe covering it that matches the Caftan. The robe is left slightly open, and a belt is fastened over it.

When I first saw a Takchita, I was amazed by the amount of detail that goes into it. Nearly every single inch of the gown has some sort of jewel or design on it. Even the belt is covered in embroidery and jewels! Also, they come in any color you can imagine, and they're often at least two colors.

Takchitas are reserved for special occasions only, most commonly weddings. At a traditional Moroccan wedding, the bridge changes into five different ones! Each one is a different color, carrying a different meaning. Guests also wear a Takchita, and may even change a few times as well.

Unlike Caftans and Jillabas, I don't recommend buying one unless you're celebrating a special occasion. They can be pricey (though you have the option to rent) and too warm for Moroccan weather. They're also very heavy!

CULTURE

48. TIGHT-KNIT SOCIETY

Something that I found to be unique about Morocco is how close everybody is. This is especially true for families, but even whole communities can be extremely close as well.

In families, there isn't much of an individualistic attitude that western countries typically have. Instead, everyone is expected to take care of each other as long as they may need it. For example, it's common for a man to live in one house with his parents, wife, children, siblings, and more. If he's unable to find a job or in a difficult financial situation, his parents will support him and his family until he gets back on his feet. Even other family members like aunts and uncles help their family frequently, especially if they're living abroad and have more money to spend. They will often send hundreds of dollars a month to their family in Morocco!

Neighbors are often close as well, especially in more rural areas. They usually get invited to big events, like weddings, births, and funerals.

Sometimes they spend a lot of time at each other's houses as well, just chatting or enjoying a meal together.

49. HOSPITALITY

One of the best things about Morocco is the amazing hospitality. If you enter a Moroccan home, one thing is for sure: You will be treated like royalty!

The most common way that Moroccans show love is through food. From the moment you arrive, they will be bringing you all sorts of different dishes, so be prepared to eat! If you're staying with them for a while, they will bring you breakfast, lunch, and dinner plus snacks and desserts until you leave. They tend to cook the fanciest meals for guests as well.

Moroccans will also let you stay with them for as long as you want or need to. If you only want to stay for 3 days, they will encourage you to stay for a week because they don't want to see you go. One of their favorite pastimes is chatting and spending time with guests.

If you're a woman, Moroccans will apply henna for you as well, since it's tradition to do it for guests. They will even sometimes give you gifts such as Jillabas, Caftans, and more. Their generosity is never-ending!

50. SLOW PACE OF LIFE

If you like to relax, you'll love Morocco! Moroccans lead a very laid-back lifestyle and have a different view of time. Even at work, it's common for people to be chatting, watching their phones, and taking frequent breaks. It's also common for people to show up late or not show up at all depending on the position.

This can be a good thing because there's less anxiety and stress, especially in the workplace. Moroccans tend to have more time to spend on themselves and their hobbies and interests than people in western countries. While in Morocco, you will see people hanging out in cafes from morning to night, talking to their friends, or doing nothing at all.

However, this can also be a bad thing sometimes. If you need something to be done quickly, expect it to take a while. For example, if you need paperwork done you will almost always be told to come back later or ask a different person. From my time living in Morocco, I learned that you just need to be patient and be affirmative when necessary.

TOP REASONS TO BOOK THIS TRIP

People: Moroccan people are some of the kindest and most generous people I've ever met. Whether you just need a hand or you need a place to spend the night, they are always here to help.

Food: After somebody visits Morocco, they'll always go on and on about how great the food is, and it's no surprise why! Moroccan food is always made fresh with a large variety of meat, vegetables, and spices.

Weather: If you like warm, sunny weather then you should definitely visit Morocco. In Marrakech, it's fairly warm all year round.

PACKING AND PLANNING TIPS

A Week before Leaving

- Arrange for someone to take care of pets and water plants.

- Email and Print important Documents.

- Get Visa and vaccines if needed.

- Check for travel warnings.

- Stop mail and newspaper.

- Notify Credit Card companies where you are going.

- Passports and photo identification is up to date.

- Pay bills.

- Copy important items and download travel Apps.

- Start collecting small bills for tips.

- Have post office hold mail while you are away.

- Check weather for the week.

- Car inspected, oil is changed, and tires have the correct pressure.

- Check airline luggage restrictions.

- Download Apps needed for your trip.

Right Before Leaving

- Contact bank and credit cards to tell them your location.

- Clean out refrigerator.

- Empty garbage cans.

- Lock windows.

- Make sure you have the proper identification with you.

- Bring cash for tips.

- Remember travel documents.

- Lock door behind you.

- Remember wallet.

- Unplug items in house and pack chargers.

- Change your thermostat settings.

- Charge electronics, and prepare camera memory cards.

READ OTHER
GREATER THAN A TOURIST
BOOKS

Greater Than a Tourist- California: 50 Travel Tips from Locals

Greater Than a Tourist- Salem Massachusetts USA 50 Travel Tips from a Local by Danielle Lasher

Greater Than a Tourist United States: 50 Travel Tips from Locals

Greater Than a Tourist- St. Croix US Birgin Islands USA: 50 Travel Tips from a Local by Tracy Birdsall

Greater Than a Tourist- Montana: 50 Travel Tips from a Local by Laurie White

Children's Book: Charlie the Cavalier Travels the World by Lisa Rusczyk Ed. D.

> TOURIST

Follow us on Instagram for beautiful travel images:
http://Instagram.com/GreaterThanATourist

Follow *Greater Than a Tourist* on Amazon.

CZYKPublishing.com

> TOURIST

At *Greater Than a Tourist*, we love to share travel tips with you. How did we do? What guidance do you have for how we can give you better advice for your next trip? Please send your feedback to GreaterThanaTourist@gmail.com as we continue to improve the series. We appreciate your constructive feedback. Thank you.

METRIC CONVERSIONS

TEMPERATURE

110° F —   — 40° C
100° F —
90° F —   — 30° C
80° F —
70° F —   — 20° C
60° F —
50° F —   — 10° C
40° F —
32° F —   — 0° C
20° F —
10° F —   — -10° C
0° F —
-10° F —   — -18° C
-20° F —   — -30° C

To convert F to C:
Subtract 32, and then multiply by 5/9 or .5555.

To Convert C to F:
Multiply by 1.8 and then add 32.

32F = 0C

LIQUID VOLUME

To Convert:.................Multiply by
U.S. Gallons to Liters................. 3.8
U.S. Liters to Gallons 26
Imperial Gallons to U.S. Gallons 1.2
Imperial Gallons to Liters...... 4.55
Liters to Imperial Gallons 22
1 Liter = .26 U.S. Gallon
1 U.S. Gallon = 3.8 Liters

DISTANCE

To convert ....Multiply by
Inches to Centimeters 2.54
Centimeters to Inches 39
Feet to Meters........................ .3
Meters to Feet 3.28
Yards to Meters 91
Meters to Yards 1.09
Miles to Kilometers 1.61
Kilometers to Miles............. .62
1 Mile = 1.6 km
1 km = .62 Miles

WEIGHT

1 Ounce = .28 Grams
1 Pound = .4555 Kilograms
1 Gram = .04 Ounce
1 Kilogram = 2.2 Pounds

TRAVEL QUESTIONS

- Do you bring presents home to family or friends after a vacation?

- Do you get motion sick?

- Do you have a favorite billboard?

- Do you know what to do if there is a flat tire?

- Do you like a sun roof open?

- Do you like to eat in the car?

- Do you like to wear sun glasses in the car?

- Do you like toppings on your ice cream?

- Do you use public bathrooms?

- Did you bring a cell phone and does it have power?

- Do you have a form of identification with you?

- Have you ever been pulled over by a cop?

- Have you ever given money to a stranger on a road trip?

- Have you ever taken a road trip with animals?

- Have you ever gone on a vacation alone?

- Have you ever run out of gas?

- If you could move to any place in the world, where would it be?

- If you could travel anywhere in the world, where would you travel?

- If you could travel in any vehicle, which one would it be?

- If you had three things to wish for from a magic genie, what would they be?

- If you have a driver's license, how many times did it take you to pass the test?

- What are you the most afraid of on vacation?

- What do you want to get away from the most when you are on vacation?

- What foods smell bad to you?

- What item do you bring on ever trip with you away from home?

- What makes you sleepy?

- What song would you love to hear on the radio when you're cruising on the highway?

- What travel job would you want the least?

- What will you miss most while you are away from home?

- What is something you always wanted to try?

- What is the best road side attraction that you ever saw?

- What is the farthest distance you ever biked?

- What is the farthest distance you ever walked?

- What is the weirdest thing you needed to buy while on vacation?

- What is your favorite candy?

- What is your favorite color car?

- What is your favorite family vacation?

- What is your favorite food?

- What is your favorite gas station drink or food?

- What is your favorite license plate design?

- What is your favorite restaurant?

- What is your favorite smell?

- What is your favorite song?

- What is your favorite sound that nature makes?

- What is your favorite thing to bring home from a vacation?

- What is your favorite vacation with friends?

- What is your favorite way to relax?

- Where is the farthest place you ever traveled in a car?

- Where is the farthest place you ever went North, South, East and West?

- Where is your favorite place in the world?

- Who is your favorite singer?

- Who taught you how to drive?

- Who will you miss the most while you are away?

- Who if the first person you will contact when you get to your destination?

- Who brought you on your first vacation?

- Who likes to travel the most in your life?

- Would you rather be hot or cold?

- Would you rather drive above, below, or at the speed limited?

- Would you rather drive on a highway or a back road?

- Would you rather go on a train or a boat?

- Would you rather go to the beach or the woods?

TRAVEL BUCKET LIST

1.

2.

3.

4.

5.

6.

7.

8.

9.

10.

NOTES